A Domesticated Primate & Anomaly Poetry
Summer Solstice 2023 publication.
All works Copyright © 2023
by the individual artists.
This collection Copyright © 2023
by Domesticated Primate

READ MORE, YOU TROGLODYTE!
This is a work of fiction. Names, characters, and incidents are either the product of the author's imaginations or are used factiously, and any resemblance to actual persons, living or dead, businesses, companies, events, or locales is entirely coincidental.
So, chill out fool.
Contact the publisher: nick@domesticatedprimate.com

RITUALS

Summer 2023

Never Before
by Sampson

A time I've never encountered before

A part of the city I've never lived in before

A job I've never done before

A parenting role I've never played before

An understanding I've never obtained before

A routine I've never used before

A style I've never developed before

Change

Change

A Memory
by Rachel Dzengelewski

Once I fell in love with a boy with a red-feathered fedora
and thrift store shoes,
a guitar, and a kiss that left me speechless.
I loved his eyes. Those eyes. Those brooding brown eyes.
One day the boy left — because we all need to.
He took his hat and his shoes and guitar and his kiss,
and he moved to
California or Oklahoma or Arizona or Maine,
and for a time I felt sad.
Then one day the boy came back.
He tried to find me and he did,
but by then I had changed — because we all need to.

Invested
by Melanie McMullin

i wish this moment could last longer
gently rocking
beneath patchy blue and white
my favorite kind of sky
the wind exhales
an involuntary shiver under my blanket
i like to hear the trees and birds
sing their songs
i like the warmth when the sun shines past the clouds
i like the shadow play on my journal
my pen rolls off the edge of the hammock
i must lean over
i know it is time
or they will be the last ones
holding hands with a teacher's aide with
somewhere else to be
their needs
my needs

Melanie McMullin

always a delicate balance
i am
a gerber daisy spreading happiness
a butterfly signaling freedom
a mystic seeing beyond the veil
a sage with deep wisdom to share
a poet expanding compassion
i cannot fit the whole of my being into a box
there is no category for me on the census form
in my own mind i cherish this about me
but
but
i force myself to rise
in time to collect
treasures i question
i am capable of safe keeping

"Sacred" by Melanie McMullin. Marker and pen on woodblock.

notes from a once cold sidewalk
by Maria Giella

Rest assured
Spring is here again

The sound of sunrise
Wakes up a neighborhood
Saffron and goldenrod skies
Canvas the sunken tired
Winter eyes
That never raised an eyebrow
Because they simply couldn't

The breath of new life
Rings true in all of us
Budding trees and walks
On the fresh pavement
Little girl's scooter wheels
Come to a brisk stop, getting caught
In a sidewalks fracture
Helmet slouches toward eyebrows
"She'll grow into it."

Dirt on hands and elbows
Gets back up again and again
Wash your hands when you
Come home

Rest assured,
Spring is here again

What Is Grace?
by Tracey Saloman

I am not aging
gracefully.
Although some say
I do it well.
I do it
in a sour mash
of resignation
resentment
and not a little fear.

Perhaps I will be
an epic vintage.

I am not aging
gracefully.
When young
women gush over
my greys, so natural
they say. "We can't wait!"
oblivious
to my narrowed stare
as if I chose
to unstopper the bleaching of time.

"You could pass for ten years younger,"
no longer means in your 20's.
Extra curves emerge in places
they have no right to be.
I'm still a handful
with a mouth full of sass.

I am not aging
gracefully.
Once a month
I curl in
on myself, crippled,
cursing and crying
popping pain killers.

Tracey Saloman

But they don't kill
the pain of knowing
always a uterus
never a womb.*

Ironically,
Love finally found me.
Desire unshakable, insatiable
ferocious in its demand
I see myself
the way he does,
not tinged with sadness
for my first life
dreams, almost
dead and buried.

I am not aging
gracefully.
There is panic
in the dark, sleepless nights
mysterious pains.
Fears of time gone
congeal in my breast
going neither up nor down.

I'm almost the age my mother was
when she died.

I am not aging
gracefully,
but it really doesn't matter.
Someday it will be here
in its wrinkled splendor
and silvered inevitability.
And I will no longer have to worry
about getting old.

*Grateful to share that two years later, I gave birth to my son, Mycah Nathaniel, on Dec 31, 2022.

Remember The Boy
by AJ

I just wanna remember the boy who's healing,
I don't want to forget who I used to be.
It wasn't that I thought I was too good, I just knew "that" life
wasn't good enough for me.
I mourn the lack of photos in my box of memories
Of that little baby boy who's knees were scrubbed
because they were turning brown

I mourn the lack of photos in my box of memories
so I frame my index and thumb around my right eye
as I squint my left,
And create a facade of frames,
and shadow boxes and books, ones that
reflect the boy in all of his looks.

In the summer time, darker melanin
My white mother ignorant of my tanning skin
She'd joke around for years after that,
And I'd never show my pride for being Puerto Rican
So, I look down at my darkening palms and
capture a picture of the little boy
caught in identity's limbo, if only just in my mind

That angel who acted too girly,
instead of holding me, they quit
He tried to play with Barbies and the kitchenette
But Abuela said thats not proper boy etiquette
So, I look on blank walls and frame a photo
of the boy who wore his aunt's communion dress
and prances down the halls, if only to reframe time

Years later, glances on buses,
so closer I sat
To the matriarch who barely wanted to meet me
Where I was growing at.
So, I glance at my phone and scroll upon
an imaginary memory of the boy's
abuela celebrating all that he was,
and the femininity
she wasn't allowed to embrace

AJ

Now that lack is her own sin to face
One side riddled with addiction
because they're trying to cope
A swig of this, a hit of that, snort this line of hope
And with that, a crumpled memory
in the corners of my ragged cork wallet,
holding space for the mommy that never was,
but had many undying chances
to be.

Here's to another made-up memory
Of the boy that was, and the love that wasn't
Daddy's side hiding generational abuse
The pain just rolled into me,
Under rugs it was swept
And I wept as the truth crept
And no one cared to intercept
Facades of forgiveness because
Their "baby jesus" told them so
So, I burn the photo of a fake Jesus.
The one whose love wasn't unconditional,
the one who was painted by a lineage of lies and decrepit men

I wasn't macho enough, and perhaps too white
A queer young boy embracing his colors,
but he looked just a little too light
But, that picture of the boy,
the one in the rose red dress,
sprawled on green and fertile grass,
waiting for the laughs to pass,
all because he just wanted to feel beautiful
That one...that one may as well be tattooed on me.
Because that boy...became
this man.

AJ

Daddy's family didn't want me,
I could never understand why
Trying to buy my love worked for a moment
Until there was nothing left to buy.
As I peered at an abundant spruce on a quiet Noche Buena,
it still encapsulated
emptiness.
Gifts were hidden, and so was daddy.

A photo of fear, did the boy do something wrong?
I snap that photo and store it in my
"to be destroyed, but never forgotten"
file in my mind's recycle bin.
This weight was never mine to carry, but the roots
sprawled deep from within.
That boy grew apart and afar and away
and the photos drifted in the wind,
astray

In someone else's basement or attic
In moldy boxes where they lay,
Faded maybe, but my desire is vivid
To meet that boy in the photos
And tell him that he kept on living.
Living through and for his own child,
a baby named Oasis.
They play pretend, and create art,
and have tea parties, and prance in dresses
and celebrate every shade of skin.

They eat arroz con pollo, and cantá en español.
Coming full circle, made the boy's life whole.
They denounce gender norms,
and patriarchy in all forms.
Their photos are captured, printed,
and hung on the walls of their home, and
not just an imaginary gallery.

He'll always remember the boy.
All because of his baby girl.

TWENTY SEVEN
by Lionel Frenchette

happy birthday
alphabetically: aabdhhipprtyy
in binary code: 1001000 1100001 1110000 1110000 1111001 1000010
1101001 1110010 1110100
1101000 1100100 1100001 1111001
to me:

one more year around the sun!
one more year alive!
one year older!
one year wiser!
every minute in the present that you are alive
is the oldest you've ever been.
every minute in the present is the youngest you can be.

my birthday present to you is...

my birthday wish is selfish.
i want to trust in love.

a mirror!

thank you, thank you.

"Cigarette Break" by Phillip J. Mellen. Paper Collage..

Cigarette Break
by Phillip J. Mellen

I remember there was a small window in her bedroom
by where she took cigarette breaks
it was a break from the madness for her,

Life wasn't always so mad
it just grew that way,

Away from the sun,
toward the moon

This is when she began.

Fatherless
by Gigi Tierney

Summer afternoon, leaning toward
Evening; I am eight and
Sitting on the stoop in self imposed exile
To escape the humid noise of family inside
That made it hard to breathe.
I never met my father but when I raged
They told me I was like him
My knees constantly bruised
From stubbornness, from going through obstacles,
Never around.
Ants crawl over my bare feet and I wonder
Could I take lickings like his other kids
If he came for me?
I wait until the light slants orange across the yard
But only mosquitos arrive.
Once I found his picture in the basement
And an old letter he wrote
Full of threats and nasty words
To my mother after she spooked-deer bolted;
Apocrypha sourcing those alien parts of me.
I immediately understand this
Is how he made sure we'd stay away for good.
Years later, I find out he died
From a half brother who says
"You didn't miss anything."

Ghost Train Trail
by Meaghan Moraes Gerzon

Damp and nearly dusk,
we set out down the trail
Where trains came through
in 1800-something
And the mills remain
as rubble.

Muslin cloths covered
the cars like ghosts
And steel made the world move
like starry eyed youth
and a good day's work.

Now we romp through gravel,
keeping the rocks in crevices
Seeing what once was
and longing for something I don't know
but can feel.
Like a ghost.

"Summer Evening at the Cafe" by Emily M. Sujka.
iPhone 13 Pro.

The Cognates of Chronos
by Emily M. Sujka

I love finding,
The aged old men,
That sit seemingly idle,
Ajar in restaurant seats.
Bench fixtures.
They have ways
Of finding the preeminence,
In the present
Of the day.
Their presence
Doesn't mask time's passing—
It joins it.
Not the protagonist
But the neighborhood pragmatist,
A cap-on participant
Party to what
Or who
Finds them
And their preoccupations;
The missus says it's veggie night,
Spinach and chickpeas.

Bridge
by Colin Williams

I listen to radio; I talk with my friends.
I read the newspaper; I watch for the crowd.

It's said that it's open: I drive there, it's not.
I hear that it's fixed; I sit and watch boats.

It's bad for the trucks; it's bad for our cars.
It's bad for their bikes; it's bad when you walk.

For those seagulls it's open; for us, it is not.

"Is it Open or is it Closed?" by James Mulvey.

The Devil's Playground
by Stephen Harrington

Welcome to the Devil's Playground
The sign says 'if you dare'
Curiosity becomes regret
As soon as you breath the air.

Beware of playing hide and seek
With demons, fiends and ghouls.
After they poke you in the eyes,
You'll be their favorite fool.

Danger is always lurking
At the bottom of the slide.
By the time you see it coming,
It's too late to save your hide.

Stay away from the sandbox,
A cruel and devious snare!
Filled to the brim with quicksand,
It's all downhill from there.

All you'll get is the run-around
Chasing shadows on a carousel.
So far behind you'll think you're first,
On a pony straight outta hell.

Goblins and gremlins will trick you,
They'll offer a push on a swing.
Say goodbye to an autumn moon,
You'll be landing sometime next spring.

There's hell to pay for admission
As it goes from bad to worse,
You're better off just to stay away
The whole damn place is cursed.

"Manic" by Harley G. French. Acrylic on canvas.

__Summertime Nights__
by Berto

The sky's bright tonight,
Dotted with twinkling light,
I can't remember the last time
They've looked so bright.

Maybe it's your spell
That's got me feeling such delight!
Or it just might be these
Damn summer time nights.

__A Night Time Ride__
by Berto

The sun has long gone down
As the sounds of the city rise up.

That ooollld feeling comes again
It jolts you wide awake.

The sounds the sights!
Yeah, it's that time again,

Time to grab the keys and ride.

Sherri's Father
by Peter M. Gordon

Me and all my fifteen-year-old friends,
Brooklyn and Queens born, found Sherri,
fifteen and a half,

honey hair, tanned skin, endlessly fascinating.
Her Valley Girl talk, dazzling braces-free smile;
her *otherness* attracted us.

How could a creature exist? And she was Jewish!
Of course we believed we loved her. So full we were
of hormones and despair.

I never thought how our constant attention
affected her, I just hoped Sherri would hold
my hand. One week, her father

Jack came to see her at our Catskill bungalow
colony, also tan and California, like a Hebrew TV
Dad, so different from our fathers.

Peter M. Gordon

Jack wore long sleeved shirts, even on humid
summer days. Watched Sherri swim, but never
jumped in the pool. One night,

while my friends hovered around his daughter,
moths on a porch light, he waved me over to a
green picnic table under a tall pine.

Full moon glowed his white shirt. I will never
forget how his dark pupils reflected moonlight,
saw his sleeves rolled up

for the first time, exposed muscled forearms.
My eyes froze on the blue number tattooed
across his right arm.

Mind flooded with a thousand questions
I could never ask. Why did he pick me from
all Sherri's suitors?

The Talmud says some questions have no answers,
just actions. That fall, I made up my mind to learn
it anyway, to shine light on Jack's darkness.

Picnic Picayune
by Frank William Finney

Enough salad here to feed a warren.
Plenty of popcorn. Plenty of beer.
Beet juice, silly. Hardly blood.
Slide the veggies off the skewer.
Care for a pickle? Sweet or sour?
Wanna try the spinach pie?
Lovely weather anyway…
Wait till you taste the watermelon!

"Come Find Me" by Kate Fraser Rego

groundless[*]

by nikki fragala barnes

water is where I'm at home, not land —
although, sometimes stone
once or twice, sand
as the wrack lines form a frown
while the moon prompts her command
erasing the shore, illegible (un)read
unspoken things,
reminding the salt and water, each fed
stroking gently or rough, bubbles appear
shifting quickly and slow, like kings
failing to perceive abundance, a kind of despair
consumes and decay(s)
hollowing the soul bare
while currents wash me away

a terminal poem after Percy Bysshe Shelley's "Ozymandias"

Specter
by S.j. Dzięgielewski

At daybreak, damp and cold,
A slow ghost floats
Over an olivine pond —
Donning a pearl gray gown,
Disappearing beyond
Reeds and rushes
Into innumerable birch, ash, oak.

A half-rotten pitch pine
Strangled by bittersweet vines
Leans on a lone weeping willow.

In the east, a great yawning sun
Transforms the dew-speckled dawn
Into a sparkling emerald spectacle,
And breaks morning chill
With screaming electrum light.

A doe peeks, wary and watchful, through a clearing.
Our eyes meet in a half-second statue-still stalemate
Before she snaps away — quick as a rifle shot.
Merely a yearling, yet wise to the ways of men.

The Promise of Pleasant Street
by Maia Livramento, "MAIZE"

A kitchen.
An olive oil atmosphere.
Humid with steam rising off of pale yellow fluffed up rice.
yellow yellow vibes.
Clara's house.
Leather strap looms,
Tiny bedrooms hide nothing.
No pomp.
All circumstance.
Doilies and funeral cards collect no dust.
Mattresses flip often.
The fair skinned and wrinkled hand of our matriarch
resting comfortably in mine,
 chubby, brown, and curious.
The sisters will all be here soon.
A melancholic memory cherished.
Polished and stored someplace dim.

Cityscapes
by Patricia Gomes

With off-white determination
and a dream of what she could be,
should be,
Queen Anne breaks through
sun-softened tar
to dance boldly,
brazenly
along the curbstone.

Summer of Happiness
by Emily M. Sujka

With pain in my thighs
and a sun beating down
my lips grow red
from chiles and lime juice,
sweetly it stings
the happiness
there is mango
balanced between my fork and teeth
but there's an extra sweet
a New York City street
and a thirst.
I find it
seltzer water
the light goes green
and I carefully twist
as mango drips down my chin
the bottle explodes
effervescently baptized
with red lips
sore in the center
hot, smiling, stinging
I'm happy to the core.

Wednesday Afternoon
by Stephanie LeBlanc

A newborn baby at my breast, the wind tickles the leaves.

Another by the water fountain, splashing curiously
and smiling.

A fence badly in need of mending looms in the distance,
a chore for another day.

Across the yard my gaze catches yours. I smile,
laugh lines at the corners of my eyes.

My body laden with desire.
A decade gone by.
My being still laden with desire.

Late Summer Night At A Beach In Fairhaven
by Rachel Dzengelewski

The sun hangs low in a purple sky and the mothers
tell their daughters not to swim.
Late summer breezes have cooled the water.
We have no towels.
You'll get too cold.
The girls run toward the open embrace of the sea – unbridled.
Splashing and laughing
they ignore their mothers and the weight of sodden clothes.
Other mothers will say, "My children would never!"
The mothers hold up their phones to capture this moment
they never want them to forget.
They lean back, pressing their elbows into the sand and they smile –
remembering
twilight dips in oceans wearing much less
with boys whose names they can't recall.
"Come back!" the mothers yell.
And the girls listen because they are cold.

Leaving Spring Behind
by Pamela Bullard

Days getting longer now
more hours in our lives;
time is what we crave.

June Solstice coming soon
opposite its winter sister
one half a year away.

Can still see the towering bushes
Blossoms pink, purple and scarlet.
Petals falling on hair and face,
like baby's eyelashes on my cheek.

Breeze blows petals
in swirling clouds
in sunset colors.

Teens run by me in a group.
No greater pleasure,
as they giggle, yell,
free and safe in their world.
They make the street their own.
The evening speaks of freedom.

Body moves forward with joy-
Sharp pleasure of
a first summery night,
tenuous, fragile.

Tomorrow, they say
a northeast wind
will blow anew.

Pamela Bullard

The heat we crave will fade,
promising to return
on the first day of June.

But for now we breathe in
sweet evening air.
Last bird calls silenced.
Light starts to fade,
as dusk falls.

II. Summer Pleasures

Three months of summer await.
In the heat, the body prospers,
goes sensual and light.

he body remembers:
salt water, sun, on skin,
lulled for a while
into Paradise.

Smoothe on sun cream,
cannot be confused
with any other scent.
Memories take us back.

The body remembers:
sounds of laughter
and splashing,
taste of an orange
on the beach.

Pamela Bullard

Time stands still
'til shadows cross the sand.
Watch marks seven P.M.
yet bathers still float and sigh,
wonder what they have done
to be so lucky.

Kids cranky, fair skin crimson.
Legs fold under them as
they are carried home.

Stay, swim, til stars come out.
Splash til diamonds
follow legs in motion
and baby jellies
are tiny lightbulbs of
phosphorous and hope.

"Nightlight Sunset" by Kylie R.. Acylics on canvas.

Beyond The Wooded Edge
by David Mello

I walked into the woods today
alone but not afraid.
Trees were full of leaves
not yet in Autumn turn.
I found a worn out path
and followed it along.
It took me by a stream
where rippling waters flow
then curve around a pond
with ducks and geese at play.

I found myself a rock
where I could sit and think.
No human sounds were heard
no voices or machines.
All that I could hear
was the sound of nature's song.
This was a pleasant walk.
In the splendor of it all,
there is another world
beyond the wooded edge.

Old Cadillac on Cottage Road
by Frank William Finney

The headlights bounced

trees with every bump.

The potholes were deep

and the ride was slow.

Half a mile in—

we saw the wolf

we've learned to see

in every woods –

The lights

in every dream.

blind strike through
by k.r. seward

folds and blows around
in dry muted crinkle
like fallen leaves
soaked in skin lotion

no one's back in a time machine
to record our landfall
or catch prime
trash talking at the fictioneers' luncheonette

watching cows from a log hewn bench
we sun without idea
of which one moos
or what that speed cop'll do
later on

Spiritualist's Summer Home
by Sarah Jane Mulvey

Languishing through an open sky
she bends low to kiss the trees goodnight.
Clouds wink across the bright eye
Everything turning to lavender and dust in the fading light.

She bends to kiss the trees goodnight.
As above, so below.
Everything turning to lavender and dust in the fading light.
the tides keep their never-ending ebb and flow.

As above, so below.
Fire and fathomless blue.
the tides keep their never-ending ebb and flow
sit, stay silent and renew.

Fire and fathomless blue.
Can I show you my favorite sunset?
here, sit with me and renew.
in this safe harbor, this sacred inlet.

Can I show you my favorite sunset?
languishing through an open sky
in this safe harbor, this sacred inlet.
Clouds wink across the bright eye.

Nostalgic Haikus
by Joseph R.

Down at the vineyard
the shadow of the lighthouse
and the ocean air

        This city is big
        although some parts are unknown
        we still try and find

                Beautiful night sky
                You see the stars flying by
                and then the big moon

Love is Stored In The Mollusk
by Sally Arizona

I will shovel up your affection

Like a mollusk.

Kissing shells! By kissing shells!

I will unearth your tenderness,

You will help me excavate the warmth

And fondness in the sand between us,

We dig and dig through the dense, damp shore,

To find our love and meaning more,

What the world could be for us,

If we followed the stardust

That illuminates the shared path we walk,

As we stroll with our shovels carried over our shoulders,

And our luminescent mollusks

To be shucked at home, wherever that may be,

Because home is the beach, the sea, the stars, and moon

As long as you're with me.

"Untitled" by Stephen Harrington. Oil on canvas.

Birch Island
by Meaghan Moraes Gerzon

We arrived by canoe,
balancing peanut butter, wheat bread,
kidney beans and ketchup
in a cooler on bouncing knees.

Shoreline in eyesight,
the wilderness family camping trip was in swing—
on an island with an outhouse,
a rough side and a sunny one, too.

Yoga mats in the clearing with the sunrise,
facing a completely new direction.
Journals by campfire and
deflated air mattresses.
We were all simmering in the adventure.

But what I remember most is that we all loved it,
despite a storm that took down the tents,
forcing relocation to the sunny side—
and a runaway chipmunk clenching the one plastic knife smeared in peanut butter
in its little rascal mouth.

We were on Birch Island together for the first time,
and it felt like magic.
Now, a painting of birch trees hangs in my living room
in the house I live in as a grown up,
and I remember the wonder of my childhood.

Summer Time Rituals
by Shashawna Santiago

Summers of my youth feel so far gone,
Blooming into adulthood has been hard.
Childhood trauma lingers on,
However, to release I let down my guard.

Though life has guided me out of New B,
I traveled far and thrived the best I could;
Knowing good and well NB is always inside me.
Portuguese gold inside my soul, as it should be.

July was my time, born of sun & sacrifice,
Not once did my mother waive her faith,
I wish I had that quality, how that'd be nice...
Back when life felt carefree and completely safe.

I am learning how to live outside of that city,
It's limits and the limitations it placed on me.
I keep my Mother alive in my memory,
Summers, never the way they used to be:

Clam cakes shared amongst aunts and cousins,
Backyard barbeques or grilling in the park,
Fort Taber or Hazelwood; linguica, jague & buns
Outside till the stars were in our eyes after dark.

Blowing bubbles, riding bikes, sidewalk chalk;
Popsicles freezing, potato salad in the fridge,
Fried chicken picnic, or fireworks by the dock.
Sitting by the "T" or the pier, living on the edge.

Cobblestone roads on the way to visit family,
Left turn arrow at the bottom of Union St.
It was one of my favorite lights to see,
Now it's gone and never again shall we meet.

Shashawna Santiago

Hot seatbelt buckles, kids packed in backseats
Camping, sleepovers or get-togethers,
Singing along to the top songs or radio beats,
Living our lives to the fullest, unaware of all hurts.

Ice cream cones down by the hurricane wall,
West beach trips with toes in the sand,
Daily exercise to keep us busy, to grow tall,
Swinging high on the swings, chains in my hand.

Summers look entirely different these days...
New England coastlines have turned into
Colorful skylines out in the country, fields of hay.
I see brown cows everyday & I think of you.
"How Now Brown Cow," we used to say,
I never thought I'd see so many in a day...

It's funny how rituals change as you age...
All of the seasons still rotate and coordinate,
The sun comes up and then goes down,
I wish youthful summers to everyone around...

Keep those sunny days in mind
Any time the world gets tough,
Remember you are born of summer sun.
Baby, you burn bright because...

You Are More Than Enough.

"Breath" by Melanie McMullin. Pencil, marker, crayon, pen, and magazine cuttings on mixed media pad.

Belong
by Mark Walsh

The swing set in the back yard
had room for five kids
but most days I swung alone.

From that swing I watched
kidfull cars drive off to
beachside amusement parks
or downtown department stores
then kicked the air
pumped my legs
traced the patch of dirt to
high pine boughs along the arc
of not being asked.

Swinging was a way of
blowing aside abandonment
a release from being
picked last or finding
yourself at a joke's
butt end.

Then that summer our neighbor's
grandkids visited for a week
we played games without captains
or blame across fenceless backyards.

At lunch time I went away
taught earlier that a place
at the table appeared
only when absence
needed a warm any body.

Mark Walsh

From my swing I watched seven
Grandchildren around a checkered
picnic table feast on hot dogs
Hamburgers potato chips
they ate and waved
I kicked against all of it
starting over.

When the grandson
my age ran to me
waving smiling wanting to know
why I was over here alone
because a plate of food
waited for me with them –

acceptance lifted me
to the ground.
The taste of belonging
lingers on my tongue.

The Crying Boy
    by AJ

I want to hold the crying boy
Who was told he was too feminine
So his father scolded him to a dark corner
Literal darkness
Figurative darkness

I want to lift his chin
And tell him he is pretty
And that crying is not weakness
And emotions show us what matters
And then bless him with glitter
The color of his choosing

I want to dance with the crying boy
While he prances around in his mama's heels
I'll grab his hand and give him a spin
"Let's hear it for the boy" will be playing
And we will be listening

I want to feed the crying boy
With the soul food of reassurance
That one day pretty and flamboyant
Will be his superpowers

AJ

I want to read to the crying boy
Tales and truths of princes and activists
Princesses and powerhouses
That came before him,
That lived before me.
So that he may know people like us
Make history.

I wanna show the crying boy
That it gets easier
And more difficult at the same time.
Our superpower is authenticity
And the people that try to tear us down
Are doing so because of their own cracking foundation.

I want to remind the crying boy
Of the person he will one day grow up to be.

So, I look into the mirror

First Second
by Joodzell Louis

Dear Her,
It's funny I never think about things like soulmate, twin flame,
or even first love when I was a kid
because I thought it was stupid
Cuz I really thought it was like a white folks things in
them white movies

I really thought it was silly because how could someone love me?
I don't dress well
my face stands still
I get annoyed easily
And I'm always second.

Well the list goes on , and on, and on
And even that time you met me you still took me in
We were like the cheetah girls, OMG Girlz , Bey & Kelly
even got my mother asking "Is Yall gay"
But listen
she didn't get us!

Joodzell Louis

We laughed , expressed our annoyance and even try to find
out where we live and this whole time
we lived up the street from each other

I could say our love resembles
a mother cutting up fruit for their child
randomly during the day
Or
A dandelion that we press against the tip of our nose
to the whispers of our mouths
Creating a wish to stay friends forever
But that didn't happen it never did.

Because you almost got me thinking having that soulmate, twin flame,
or even first love almost never ends
like them white movies.

But
Thank you for being my first
My first friend
My first love
My first everything

Because of course after everything that you made
 first went and turned me into a second

Winter's Loss
by Linda Orr

Hard seed
Softens to bud
awakens to bloom
petals fall, leaving thorns.

Discovery of new love,
playful joy,
a waterfall of longing
yet
Will he hurt me?

Does winter eventually follow spring?
warm summer caresses
turn the waterfall into a sultry flowing river.
Sparkling fresh water, and the
cold curl of the fiddlehead turns to the silken graze of the fern.

yes, the cold of winter's loss will come
after the warm breeze of summer's ease.
If we shy away from the sorrows of tomorrow
we'll miss the promise of bliss.

Take the risk.
Loving is worth the loss it holds.
Every time
Every time.

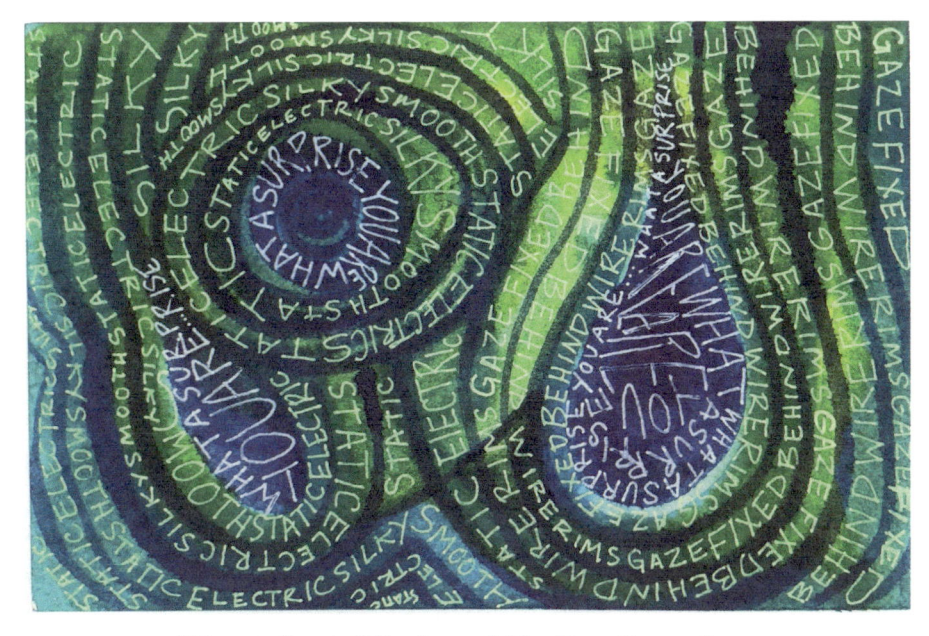

"Electric Static Silky Smooth" by Kate Fraser Rego.
Acrylic & mixed media on canvas.

Le Parole Non Dette*
by Roberto Marzano

Le parole non dette
muoion d'arsura, di fremiti
vespai di cupa inquietudine
perdono fiato, e più sillabe
diventan pietre allo stomaco
balbettii incespicanti
nei circospetti silenzi
scemano stupidamente
dimenticando esse stesse
per chi non fu quel "ti amo"
o il soffocato "ti odio"
autoingoiatosi vile.

*presented side-by-side in the author's native Italian,
and his English translation on the opposite page.*

The Unspoken Words
by Roberto Marzano

The unspoken words
dying of heat, of shudders
crawl spaces of gloomy uneasiness
lose breath, and more syllables
they become stones in the stomach
stammering stumbling
in circumspect silences
stupidly fade
forgetting themselves
for those who were that "I love you"
or the suffocated "I hate you"
cowardly self-swallowing.

Oak Tree
by Stephen Harrington

Together beneath an oak tree
We sheltered from the rain
After a pledge of unity
We carved each other's name

With a heart an an arrow
Our sincerity was sealed.
In the magic of that moment
Loving feelings felt so real.

Sparks became a burning flame
Rising higher and higher
No rain from the heavens
Could ever put out that fire.

We turned lightning to thunder
A breath to a moan
We held hands in silence
As we made our way home.

In our hearts we both knew
This was no summer fling.
The magic of autumn
Turned to winter, then spring.

Anniversaries yet come
Like a warm gentle breeze
On that day every summer
When love was conceived.

Observances
by Mark Walsh

Thoreau knew an anthill could provide
an afternoon's entertainment. Back much
further, twelve-year-olds were sent by parents
to gather acorns for the tribe. One summer
resort day my buddy and I let our suburban minds
hatch a swell idea: grab up the day-glo coffee
cans repurposed as lounge chair ashtrays,
dump them in the creek that ran under the cement
Swimming pool and watch them tumble down
the short falls inside the tree line. A good
hours' amusement before we got nabbed,
loudly lectured, made to climb down slippery stones
and gather up every dented can in our stubby reach.
A large crowd enjoyed the justice. Later, we shrugged
it off with a laugh, blind to the real crime. *People of*
wilderness cultures rarely seek out adventures.*
Boredom is the god that gets us in the end.

*line in italics is borrowed from an essay by Gary Snyder,
found in "The Practice of The Wild"

no one remembers
by k.r. seward

those four years before

five years after

three years in some location

if they did

we're just as old

and dead

or alive

down the line

wayward slots to sift down into

all over for so many

even those remembered

not just us

in dashed up passage lines

k.r. seward

we come

and go

perhaps to linger

because someone remembers

even if they really do recall you

pain gathers too high

to hold on

tears won't water much

thin salted streams

no good for any growing

better buried

and not showing

next spring or summer

who can bring on flowers enough

Fulll Moon
by Sarah Jane Mulvey

I am small beneath her violet glow,
Staring up, asking, pleading.
She knows the tides of my body,
The blue-black movements in my core.

She hears the rain-soaked Earth
that calls her home,
Feels the pull of his vast ocean,
but she will not be moved.
How can I be like her?
Waxing and waning, but never despairing.

To smell the green of the world returning,
feel the last efforts of the sun.
Smell the fires burning,
I wonder how long.

The thunderous moon,
The pull of life.
Steadfast, yet ever changing.

"Brooklyn Bel Air" by Emily M. Sujka. iPhone 13 Pro

For Olivia from Escanaba
by Peter M. Gordon

Olivia, if only I could hold your nicotine-stained
hand one more time while we sneak cigarettes
behind that boat house on the Manistique River.
That summer we promised to make out only
as practice for future boyfriends and girlfriends,
afraid to go too far past second base without
birth control. Trembling from fear of our futures
and desire for flesh, exchanged smoky kisses,
kept clothes on while we explored body parts.
Afterward waded into the river to hide
embarrassing stains. What shame made us
fear feelings, hide them from friends, family,
who surely knew? If I could whisper into my
teenage ear today, I'd tell him, "Wring every
last drop of joy from this rag of life,"

Wrote each other that fall, for a while.
She sent love notes on pink paper, scented
with perfume and tobacco smoke.

I can't remember when or why
we stopped writing. It's like trying
to remember falling asleep.

Stolen Voices
by Anisa Tavares

quiet whispers in the dim of the dark;
she looks at me and says
"do you love me or not?"

how could i possibly tell you
when my voice you have taken,
among many other things, too.

she's so incredibly enchanting,
sitting there without a clue in the world.
my whole self to her i wish to be granting.

like two pieces of puzzle, yet
from opposite sides of the board,
nevertheless such an asset.

"my love for you remains ever so steady."
i tell her seriously, she giggles and says
"you used that one already."

she starts to disappear into the night's huff,
as she always does.
no love confession ever seems to be enough

to get her to stay.

How To Build A Shadow
by Kae Winter

I think of it in the back of her throat
just before the sun rises, walking toward the horizon
the long journey down the center of her damp tongue

        "Is this where we start?"

A darkness so free of light, it touches light
stretches like tree branches
slapping the windows of her house at dusk with demands
so subtle, she slides her bones inside me silently
while they slither in through the cracks in the blinds
finding form like vines climbing her bedroom walls
and our bodies;
swallowing each other
before we know they want to come inside;
grow inside us. Clinging to our ribs
like children in cages long for return to their familiar

        "Is this where we begin?"

A snake wraps its smooth scales like desire
around our necks
her teeth penetrate and a solid white ghost becomes nothing more than
spilled milk left unaffected, unexamined
only a new story, a new spot to clean up, to remove

        "Is this where we start?"

Kae Winter

At the losing of the daylight
body becoming blurred, in the distance I think I can
see her. I swear she sings to me while I'm here
her voice stays in the floorboards like phantom cries
from the spaces where my child
learns to fit in the world, outside of me

    "This house was built in 1910, I want you here with me."

She says, opening my body like a tomato sauce jar
that's sat unbothered behind the others; back corner of
the pantry, where she goes to shed her skin four times each year
The unswept corners, dust like dancing, uninhibited by feet

    "Is this where she starts?"

The light taunts us from inside, her torches lit along the
walkway to the back door
while I swallow the giant fiery ball, burning holes in my cheeks
her skin lay there next to the years of too much exposure
ashes to ashes, dust to dust
falling around the floors of her home I sleep in sometimes
weeping or glistening like ornaments forgotten on a Christmas
tree left without water. Still, its branches--
dried needles, dead, things without life
block the light just the same
stretching its exhausted arms toward me
while I tiptoe, tiptoe, tiptoe
waiting for her to reach
as I hum along
hurriedly before the night calls, again

building our home at the edge of a shadow.

Leaving Our Home
by Kae Winter

Just like when you opened your eyes
that day you were born, I sat legs-crossed
arms open with eager need, to hold
one thousand years before—
the waiting, just like that day
you ran
your fingers along the rough cedar floorboards
of your childhood home, innocence splintered
that night on your front porch
finding what you didn't want in the mouths
of teen-aged boys, one thousand years before
your lips fell on my shaky fingertips
found softly in the grooves of my spine, the feeling, again

of home.

I heard your thoughts somewhere far away, fall from
pine needles at 3 am, pointed descent to the darkness
the gritted Forest floor, I was awoken by a cricket
stuck in the wall of my living room
then, rocking the chair that I'd learned to be alone in,
the company of the creaking, crackling
of the fire, the embers and soot shadow-danced
a memory of you along the hallway walls, most nights
in the house we
forgot to live in, one thousand years before
the ghosts we became
in each other's bodies, the skin we left hanging
to dry, the passion we burned up, branded
our organs with the need, in your absence
the lost air forces me to breathe, one thousand years before
ashes finding new form, leaving their mark
on the cedar floorboards, that day you
started leaving our home.

Picking Thru The Ruins
by Pamela Bullard

Picking through the ruins of their lives,
no archeologist looking for shards,
just a bystander among the wreckage
of my sister's existence.
A lonely witness sifting thru the remains
of a time when hope reigned.
The girls were bright and beautiful,
the parents snug in the devotion,
of neighbors and family.

I cradle the 2009 statue in my arms
inscribed to "Sarah, the healer."
Her husband Bob had made it for her.
A woman holds the head
of a weakening man in her lap.
His death has already been announced;
she is the healer who will keep him alive,
with his fierce iron will, for six more years.

On the walls, posters and photos of
daughters Vanessa, Nicole, Ashey.
Even their names spoke of promise:
weddings, births, graduations.
I trace the face of the deceased
with my finger
as he holds his first daughter
at birth, no greater joy.

All the remains of the brick tudor house
In D.C. lie strewn on beds and floors.
The home of thirty years lost to unemployment
and money frittered away in the everyday
'till there was nothing.

The rocking chairs from which they watched
their daughters play,

Pamela Bullard

the long-broken grandfather clock
still majestic in a corner,
painted with the suns and moons
which marked the hours of their lives.

On the closet floor, wrinkled and faded,
stubs of fat paychecks from the good years.
An old list, streaked with tears of what they'd lost:
twenty names and twenty numbers, twenty families
on the blocks near the old brick Tudor
who shared it all.
From child care to rotating pot luck dinners,
it was a place where they felt safe.
Someone always had your back.

Eight years ago, the forced move
to a tiny rental, surrounded by strangers.
Another state, another town, another life.
Most of the cases of books, paintings,
sofas and chairs gone now,
sold or given away, lost or broken.

Evidence of two people's job searches
piled by the computer.
Resumes to make yourselves look good,
 look young, look professional.
The searches started after the jobs
promised when they had moved
were lost in the first year, one by one.

Pamela Bullard

Hundreds of letters written,
notebooks full of offers and rejections.
 Start ups opened and closed,
giving slim hope for a few months.
 No final paychecks were sent,
 as bankruptcy was declared.

Hanging in the bedroom, the party dresses
and silk shirts for dinners, dances.
The suits for him, suits for her
for all the years of meetings and travel
with the Department of Commerce for her,
Exxon Mobil and Houghton-Mifflin for him.

On the floor a faded baseball cap marked
"Dysfunctional Vietnam Veteran."
Sarah had held it in her hands for a moment
and wondered why
the chemicals sprayed in that long ago war
had killed the enemy
had killed our own
had left her abandoned.
He died too soon.

Brothers of the Sword
by David Mello

I walk among the fallen
who lay beneath the grass.
Rows of granite headstones
stretch far beyond the eye.

Yellow flowers neatly placed
in designs that speak of peace.
No one famous rests here
just soldiers from the ranks.

Battle sounds I hear
from lands so far away.
Few can tell the story
of how they met their end.

No arms were there to comfort them
when they trembled from the fear.
Their thoughts were not of glory,
but of loved ones to be near.

Their final words silenced
by the raging sounds of war.
Their souls placed by God
in the hall of fallen heroes.

Cannon stand in silence now,
the bugle calls them home.
May they never be forgotten
these brothers of the sword.

Moving
by Betty Jeanne Nooth

Moving through the seasons is a matter of days,
one after another;
It's Summer again!

Solace of sun and beach replace the cold hard winter
Of losing and saying goodbye;
the last Thanksgiving, Christmas, New Year...

Spring came: the day at the canal, laying ashes to rest.
Time now...to rest too and renew, to begin again
To move, from loved one here to loved one there.

Begin again, this new and altered life.

Curling Inward
by Linda Orr

The breath comes in
and sighs out
like the ocean tide.

The wave comes into the shore
and feeds the earth.

Seawater sparkling green,
rustling stones and shells as it
flows out to renew and mend
building in strength; promising
to return and nurture again and again.

As we continue living in the ebbing and the flowing,
as we age, inexorably tiring and slowing.

As rose petals bloom, crinkle and fall
our bodies stiffen, become rigid and small
and yet our minds soften
allowing for differences, holding emotion gently
loving all.

"Curling Inward" by Linda Orr. Oil on canvas.

Travelling Light
by nikki fragala barnes

I don't remember how the conversation began, my dad already living in my house, counting his days, moving from bed to chair to porch to chair — somehow either I (or my son) brought a book down for him — a YA-pop-fiction-page-turner, The Fault in Our Stars, and he read it, dying during that month

// three years and two months after he died, I didn't bring anything with me but five days of clothes, evacuating the (living) members of my family ahead of a late summer hurricane— I must have lent that book to someone and never got it back — driving away

// I left wedding albums, plaster prints of small hands, rocks and metal of all kinds because there's nothing else in my house I care to save.

Joe
by Bruce Nunes

In Memory of Joseph F. Rapoza, III

Joe and I,
would sometimes stand
outside Gallery X,
or
at other gigs
between his sets
of progressive jazz.
Under the stars,
we would chat
while I mostly listened.

I didn't always catch what Joe would say--
I couldn't hear everything.
He didn't care
as it never stopped our talking.

And what Joe did,
was make me grin,
then chuckle;
I'd always walk away feeling good--
something I wish life, itself, could do for me.

Bruce Nunes

As a fellow trumpeter,
I was aware Joe's form was often loose;
yet more importantly,
his instrument
became an extension of his body
and his personality--
something I never accomplished--
so Joe played on and on
while I stopped.

We all miss Joe,
he was positive force
in the community and the arts.
I can still hear and see Joe playing,
and I catch myself smiling
and it makes me feel better
especially in the crescendo of night.

Unseasonable

by Jayne Renaud

Weightless, rocking in the shallow surf
Skin warming in the early summer sun
I had memorized the lines beside your closed eyes
One corner of your mouth hinting at a smile
Now the sky has filled with smoke

A chaotic wind blew up all around us
Our fingertips missed then lost each other again
My bones rebel, my body brittle
Could I have aged 20 years in just five?
My dreams are full of ghosts

You couldn't see me
My panicked arms thrashing, my voice
caught in my throat, *please*
I wax philosophical at my own grave
The cause of death was hope

Struggles
    by Sherry Grant *and Paul Cordeiro**

Independence Day
Mother says it's time
to move out

the firefighter chef
works a double shift

flying colours
in school reports
still homeless

a colony of bees
rides the whaleboat captain's
museum roses

wax statues imitate
and intimidate

nation building
on the backs of workers
slaves and immigrants

    *a rengay or "linked poem" is a collaborative effort between the two authors. Sherry's stanzas are in standard typeface, Paul's are italicized.

"Life's Choice" by Charlotte Sylvia. Acrylic on canvas.

When the Flame of The Matriarch Goes Out*
by Tracey Saloman

There is no handbook for how to
watch someone
die.

Give birth
Raise children
Save your marriage
Save your job
Save your sanity
Grieve

Life directed:
a Multi-Million dollar excuse
for minding someone else's
business.

But no one tells you
what to do
when you're sitting and waiting and watching.
There isn't a time I don't see
her white hair
her glasses
her soft cheeks
her lips thin, naked of color
the hint of weariness as she carried the weight
of my grandmother's legacy:
the matriarch.

But when someone had to do it,
she was there.
A figurehead
A torch
A touchstone
to draw the sprawling young clan together

Thanksgiving
Hannukah
Passover

Tracey Saloman

Until we grew too far
apart, in more ways
than geography.

And the flame sputtered a little.

I don't remember
when I realized she was the last of her kind.
When she was gone,
we would huddle
around the lights of our own small tribes,
digital substitutions.

Once I asked her how her marriage lasted
so long, to avoid mistakes
I might make one day.

Now, her words of wisdom —
the words that meant nothing
to a teenager —
drop
into my head
rippling, expanding.

She asked me,
*"What are you doing to help plan
your sister's wedding?"*

*"Not a thing she doesn't ask me.
I'm keeping my mouth shut this time."*

"Good." she told me. *"You've finally learned something."*

There is no handbook for how to
watch someone
die or what to do
while you wait to pass
the torch.

**for my aunt, Sybil Saloman, who became the matriarch of the
Saloman clan upon the passing of my grandmother.*

Untitled
by Sally Arizona

The capricious Cupid–
Valentine by name– watches my
peril with glee. For he would see
my ruin not as failure, but
as the most successful passion of his efforts;
ethereal love uncontainable by
mortals, ecstasy only swallowed
in the life hereafter, the skies above.
He would see it as his only
                        Saintly
              v i c t o r y.

"Amor Fati" by Kayla Conner. iPhone 13.

Amor Fati
by Kayla Conner

Love of fate
Scribbled on a bicycle in pink paint
Youthful plans slip away like sand
As the tide pulls me in too deep.
I am a horizontal Sisyphus
Stuck in liminal space.

The best laid plans they say,
I love to marinate in them, steeped tea cold from neglect.
Turn it 'round and scry into the edges.
I know the feeling is what matters. But I sit, and stew.
As if the hundredth time I turn over this rock it'll bleed.
I'll see something new.

There must be a way out of uncertainty.
Shuffle the cards again. And again.
Following shadow puppets down dark hallways
desperate for direction.
It's a fool's errand.
External projections provide no Truth.

Kayla Conner

The way out is within.
Will I drown? No matter.
Standing still is death, too.
So I strike down self doubts. They're kindling for the fire.
Dancing in the flames as they lick my fears away.
Lighting a torch and raise it high to see
The brightest light and darkest shadow. Together as always. Inside of me.
Acceptance of what is and faith at what will be.

Let go of the old roles.
Make room for miracles.
Out of darkness we rise anew ready and willing,
knowing that the past is proof
There's nothing I can't handle, nothing to stop me.

Life springs from black dirt fertilized by broken dreams.
Open to the Real. Open. Open.
A blue rose with thorns. A garden full of them.
The soul is singing
Let It Be.
Amor Fati.
Love all that comes, unconditionally.

Indelible Code
by Melanie McMullin

i am calling to you
both day and ardent night
a slow burning star with a tender core
i see the signs
on some level of inferno
your internal compass senses me
do i show up as a luscious dream
a sideways glance from unseen eyes
an intrinsic taste left on your tongue
a lingering perfume you have yet to fully inhale
elusive incandescent unforgettable
i send you arcana images in a secret language
our hearts speak in indelible code
for they are eternally knotted
as we walk through space and time
this is not a game to me
though it is fun to play with you
i watch read maybe even misinterpret
but i stay hopeful you receive the beat of my pulse
through the collective lightening we share
as we wish with fervour under the same enigmatic sky
i wonder how many moons pass
before our stars collide
and finally inevitably collapse in each other's words
held in the arms of joy

Ephemera
by S.j. Dzięgielewski

I didn't know I'd sleep
With pillows as proxy for your body over a decade after.

When I said, "Forever,"
The sort of liquor-sodden promise young men make,
I didn't know I really meant it.

And what a shame
That the cherry blossom beauty of our bare bodies
Intertwined on balmy summer nights
Would be pissed down the drain.

I didn't know I'd ache
Long after I'd forgotten the geometry of your face.

Even with another
Who desperately sewed, stitched, and sutured
Trying to close those old cuts shut,

S.j. Dzięgielewski

Even with another who is better, kinder than you.
I feel forever severed:
An amputee—
You, the phantom limb I still feel.
I'm the Androgyne Zeus cleaved in two.

Or perhaps I'm hot-pink-drunk
On banal sentiment,
Nostalgia, and staccato
Silver Screen memories
Projecting summer sun at our backs,
Stretching bent inkblot black yards beyond us.

Blissfully oblivious to the tide behind
Erasing every step we stamped in sand.
We were too young to know we never had a chance.

Weekly Ritual
by Katherine Gregory

Wednesday nights were our nights
Until you decided they weren't

Now they're just normal nights for you
But I'm waiting for them to be ours again

Snow days used to be our days
Until you decided they weren't

Thankfully we only had one this year
So it didn't hurt as bad

Homemade edibles used to be our vice
Until you decided they weren't

That's why they're still sitting on top of my fridge
Old, dried out, and smelling of stale plants

Valentine's Day was our holiday
Until you decided it wasn't

I was always the one who cooked
But I won't make heart shaped pizzas alone

Horror Story used to be our show
Until you decided it wasn't

I've stopped watching it
It's boring when you're not scaring me each week

Katherine Gregory

This shouldn't come as a surprise to you
Since I've already told you everything
While our feet stuck to the dried up booze
On the floor of the bar we're too old to be at

You held me through my tears and sobs
Knowing this is the most vulnerable I've ever been
You told me we were still best friends
And that we always will be

I stupidly believed you that night
Because the bartender had a healthy pour
And it was after the stroke of midnight
And you texted me the next morning

If anything was going to change, that would've done it
But apparently it didn't
So I have to put up a wall again
Because I can't let you close

I've stopped looking at Snapchat throwbacks
And hidden you on Instagram
Because I don't want to relive our old memories
And I don't want to see your new ones

Wednesday nights were our nights
But now I've decided they're not.

Reflections of Red
by Anisa Tavares

i'm in his eyes
that may never see,
but with, cannot feel,
is entirely impossible.
sunstreaking reflections
of red in the sky.

black so daunting
against the early morning sky,
or a late night field,
so vast and so wide,
with its speckled hidden stars
to protect a life worth living.

breathless nights chasing sleep,
so desperate to dream.
stolen air when thought of,
wonders of real life and fiction.
tears of joy when appropriate,
tears of sadness only when necessary.
all i long for is your touch,
envelope me in your scent,
so strong yet so secret.

kiss me and make me forget
everything i ever knew i knew.

the only idea i may ever have
is the idea of you against my lips,
if you'll only allow.
here for you, for you to claim stake.
i won't be angry,
for i can't feel anything at all,
unless it is admirable admiration,

for you,
and your reflections of red
in the midnight sky.

Lifesavers
by Patricia Gomes

Butter-rum sunset
and a lone cricket's song
held us captive
on a shaky fire-escape.
The blanket under us nubby and cat-furred;
we didn't mind.
We waited for the stars to come out,
forgetting how few can really be seen
above industrious city lights;
we didn't mind.
The stars, reduced in number, are easier to count.
We made it to six before we peppermint-breath kissed,
coated in the cherry-red light
from the blinking OPEN sign
of the Chinese restaurant
across the alley.

You & I
by Lionel Frenchette

like a whalefall
picked away
by hungry things

like a shipwreck
a new lightless reef
patiently eroding

i think we are cut from the same cloth
the same hard whale eye rusting
the same soft body of a ship rotting

and because we are the same
i know you are laying there dreaming
of the tenderness of being found
ready and eager to fall apart

Friends, poets, artists:
Thank you for your work
and for another stunning
edition of RITUALS.

Made in the USA
Columbia, SC
18 June 2024